Procrastination

----- ◈◈◈ -----

How to Overcome Procrastination, Master Your Life, Boost Your Productivity and Income, Be Happier and Fulfilled

**By
Nathan Ferrari**

Table of Contents

Introduction 1

Chapter One: Benefits of Overcoming Procrastination 3

Chapter Two: Underlying Cause of Procrastination 7

Chapter Three: Ways to Beat Procrastination 11

Chapter Four: Ways To Enhance Productivity 17

Conclusion 25

© Copyright 2017 by Nathan Ferrari - All rights reserved.

This document is geared towards providing exact and reliable information in regards to the topic and issue covered. The publication is sold with the idea that the publisher is not required to render accounting, officially permitted, or otherwise, qualified services. If advice is necessary, legal or professional, a practiced individual in the profession should be ordered.

- From a Declaration of Principles which was accepted and approved equally by a Committee of the American Bar Association and a Committee of Publishers and Associations.

In no way is it legal to reproduce, duplicate, or transmit any part of this document in either electronic means or in printed format. Recording of this publication is strictly prohibited and any storage of this document is not allowed unless with written permission from the publisher. All rights reserved.

The information provided herein is stated to be truthful and consistent, in that any liability, in terms of inattention or otherwise, by any usage or abuse of any policies, processes, or directions contained within is the solitary and utter responsibility of the recipient reader. Under no circumstances will any legal responsibility or blame be held against the publisher for any reparation, damages, or monetary loss due to the information herein, either directly or indirectly.

Respective authors own all copyrights not held by the publisher.

The information herein is offered for informational purposes solely, and is universal as so. The presentation of the information is without contract or any type of guarantee assurance.

The trademarks that are used are without any consent, and the publication of the trademark is without permission or backing by the trademark owner. All trademarks and brands within this book are for clarifying purposes only and are the owned by the owners themselves, not affiliated with this document.

Introduction

I would like to thank you for purchasing this book.

Putting off a seemingly easy task will make it hard and putting off a difficult task will make it impossible. Procrastination is a basic human tendency, and everyone tends to do this. We tend to keep putting things off because we don't want to do them, the task is quite annoying, or because other things need to be taken care of. At times, it can feel quite overwhelming even to start something. Other times, we tend to tell ourselves that some time and space will help in getting a better perspective of things. This is just a part of basic human nature. On the downside, procrastination can leave you feeling overburdened, discouraged and it can take a toll on personal and professional aspects of your life. Well, you don't have to worry about this, and it can be fixed by making a couple of changes to your daily schedule.

In this book, you will learn to identify the underlying causes of procrastination, the benefits of overcoming procrastination, tips for beating procrastination and some simple changes that can help in improving your overall productivity. So, why don't we get started without any further ado?

Chapter One:

Benefits of Overcoming Procrastination

Procrastination is a basic human tendency, and it is quite normal. Most don't pay much heed to it, but procrastination can prove to be quite troublesome. When you overcome procrastination, then you will be able to do the following.

Achieving your goals

Procrastination can act as a great hurdle when you are trying to achieve your goals or dreams. There might be a lot of things that you want to accomplish. However, you might be putting these off for one reason or another, and by overcoming procrastination, you will be a step closer towards achieving your goals.

Tapping into your full potential

Procrastination stops you from unlocking your true potential. Pursuing your goals and doing meaningful work that will help you in moving closer to your goals will help you in understating your real potential and realize what you are capable of. Procrastination will always prevent you from tapping into your full potential, and you will end up settling for far less than what you can do. By overcoming procrastination, you will be able to tap into the potential that is lying dormant within you.

Increases your self-control

Procrastination will certainly convince you that you are supposed to get started with work only when you feel like it. However, if you want to achieve the goals you have set for yourself, then you will need to start actively working towards them, regardless of whether you feel like doing it or not! When you start doing what you are supposed to do, without the desire to put it off, that's when, you start developing self-control.

Fewer opportunities are missed

You tend to miss out on possibilities when you procrastinate. Most of the opportunities that come your way tend to have an expiration date affixed to them. If you don't act on them immediately, those opportunities will be lost. Procrastination creates indecisiveness. If you procrastinate for a while, then the decision will be made for you, and this doesn't necessarily have to be in your favor. When you aren't a slave to procrastination, you will be able to grab all the opportunities that come along your way.

Trustworthiness

Procrastination usually gets in the way of something that you are doing. You probably made a promise to your manager that you will deliver something on time and procrastination stopped you from doing so. Over a period, this would erode the trust others have in you. You can start earning the confidence of others by beating procrastination.

Chapter One: Benefits of Overcoming Procrastination

Preventing the amplification of problems

A small problem is quite similar to a small tear in a garment. If this tear isn't fixed in time, it will become a gaping hole. Procrastination amplifies a problem. A simple error can turn into a crisis. When you stop procrastinating, you will be able to prevent the amplification of problems.

Overcoming procrastination will certainly work in your favor. Read on to learn the different ways in which you can overcome procrastination.

Chapter Two:

Underlying Cause of Procrastination

Procrastination is a common habit, and it can be quite harmless since some seem to thrive on the stress of putting things off until the deadline. However, if left unchecked, procrastination can become a serious problem, and it can throw your life out of whack. You might want to overcome procrastination if you notice that you keep missing your deadlines, or that your grades are slipping because you keep putting off your assignments until the last minute. You can break this habit right now if you want to. You can start by making a list of what the things you do when you procrastinate and then dig a little deeper to figure out the reason for this behavior. It is easier to tackle a problem when you are aware of its underlying cause.

The act of intentionally putting something off for a later date even though it should be done right away is known as procrastination. Not all procrastination is negative. For instance, if you rush off to your yoga class before starting a new project at work, it will make you feel energetic for the new challenge. Maybe you like cleaning and organizing your room before you start studying. These habits are not negative and will help in preparing yourself for the challenge that lies ahead. However, if procrastination is wreaking havoc on your personal and professional life, then it obviously isn't constructive. Once you have decided whether it is constructive or destructive, you will need to identify the underlying cause of procrastination. Here are the most common reasons.

Drama:

It can be quite exciting to procrastinate, waiting until the very last minute to complete a task can feel like you are gambling against all the odds. You are betting on yourself that you will be able to pull it off and the things that aren't in your control (reaction of your coworkers, the copy machine, or even the highway traffic), will work in your favor. So, procrastination can create drama in your life that might make things seem interesting, and this might feel better than going about doing things promptly.

The fear of failure:

If you wait until the very last to perform a task, then you can always claim that you could have done better had there been more time. Procrastination helps in providing yourself with an excuse when things don't work in your favor.

Fear of success as well:

Being afraid of success is quite real. Maybe you are worried that your responsibilities will increase if you perform well. This fear might deter you from performing well. In fact, you are effectively sabotaging yourself and your career.

Perfectionism:

You are your worst enemy. Trying to be a perfectionist will prevent you from completing a task. It is almost impossible to live up to the standards that you have created for yourself, and this will demotivate you from even starting.

Hostile feelings towards someone:

Perhaps you resent the person that assigned you the work, and by procrastinating you are simply channelizing your hostility towards them. When you don't like who you work for, it is very likely that you won't want to do the things assigned by them.

Lack of interest:

Perhaps the task that you are asked to do is boring, or it doesn't interest you. Or maybe you don't have any personal interest vested in its outcome or result.

Task seems confusing:

Maybe you don't understand something about the task on hand. Or maybe it seems unmanageable and you don't know where to start from or even how to organize it.

It is important to determine the reason for procrastination. Once you know the reason, you can try to rectify it.

Chapter Three:

Ways to Beat Procrastination

Procrastination can strike anyone at any time, and once it manages to get a firm grip on you, it can be difficult to break free of it. Even a person who is highly productive cannot escape procrastination. The key to being productive is the ability to stop yourself from giving into procrastination. Don't let procrastination stop you from working effectively and efficiently. If you want to beat procrastination, then you will need to identify the reason for doing so. Contrary to popular opinion, procrastination and laziness aren't synonyms. Procrastination stems from any negative thought or emotion that you might be harboring. When you feel like not doing something, then it is very likely that you will keep putting it off until the "right" mood strikes you. This will do you more harm than good. In this chapter, you will learn about the different strategies that you can make use of for overcoming procrastination.

Understand the reason

Do you ever feel like you aren't in the right mood to do something? Well, this feeling is nothing but procrastination that's willing you to take a break. It doesn't matter what the task at hand is, it could be something incredibly simple or even complicated. The reason for postponing what is to be done can

Procrastination

be quite varied. Instead of feeling frustrated and blaming it all on procrastination, you should instead take a moment to calm down and evaluate the situation rationally. Give yourself a while to understand the reason for procrastinating. This is the first step if you want to overcome procrastination. The information provided in the previous chapter will help you with this. Procrastinators usually concentrate on short-term gains instead of long-term gains. You should focus on the benefits of completing a task if you want to overcome procrastination. For instance, if you are putting off cleaning your bedroom, then think about how good you will feel when the room is free of all clutter, and you are lying down on your bed with fresh sheets, in a room that is clean!! This feeling will make it easier to get things done.

Getting rid of the obstacle

Before you get started with a task, take a couple of minutes and take into consideration all the possible obstacles that you might run into. Once you know what you will be up against, you can start devising a plan for avoiding or even overcoming these barriers. For instance, you have received an email giving particular instructions regarding the execution of a task according to certain instructions. It is very likely that you will keep going back to that email while working to check the instructions and this will just cause unnecessary distractions. Instead, you should just print these instructions beforehand. Plan to avoid procrastination.

Just get started

At times, it might seem difficult to take the first step, to just start something. Taking this first step might feel tough, regardless of the task at hand. Just make the first move, and it gets better from there. When you stop focusing on all the negative aspects of a given thing or situation, then you can prevent negative feelings creeping in. Just dive right in, and this will not let all those negative feelings take root. Also, at times starting a task does help in bringing about a positive outlook towards it.

Break it down

If something seems intimidating to you, it is highly probable that you will end up putting it on hold for as long as you possibly can. If you can reduce this intimidation quotient, it will be easier to work on something. The sheer size of a project can be intimidating at times. So, try and break it down into smaller parts. When you do this, the intimidation quotient will decrease. It is easier to tackle smaller tasks.

The right environment

Working in the wrong environment will pave the way for procrastination. You certainly won't be able to get any work done if you are working in a place with blaring music while your friends are sitting with you, or you are constantly on your phone checking the latest social media updates. You certainly will not be able to get any work. Your surroundings should encourage you to work.

Rejoice in the small victories

Always enjoy your successes, big or small it doesn't matter. A sense of accomplishment will help you to keep going. This will help in developing a positive attitude towards your work and will provide you with the necessary motivation to keep going. Striking off simple things from your to-do list can be quite satisfactory. If you like making to-do lists, then you will certainly understand the happiness of striking things off from that list.

Always be realistic

When you are setting goals for yourself, make sure that the goals are realistic and attainable. You will be setting yourself up for failure if you set unrealistic goals. This will increase the negative feelings, and you will ultimately succumb to procrastination.

Self-talk

The more you keep telling yourself that you aren't supposed to think about something, the more time you will spend thinking about it. This is how the human psyche tends to work. It becomes almost impossible to not think about it! The trick is not to let this happen. When you feel yourself leaning towards postponing something for a while, you should try and avoid it. Just shift your attention towards something else. For instance, instead of thinking that you aren't supposed to procrastinate, try thinking about how good you will feel once you have completed the task. In this manner, you will be able to take the necessary action instead of worrying about a certain behavior.

Don't chase perfection

Don't try to be a perfectionist all the time. It is a good thing that you want to perfect a task, but perfectionism isn't an ideal mentality to function with. The "all or nothing" sort of thinking will let procrastination sneak up on you. A perfectionist always believes that there are only two possible outcomes in any given situation, either success or failure. This isn't how the world works. It is great that you want to be good at something, but it is equally important to understand where

Chapter Three: Ways to Beat Procrastination

to draw the line as well. Don't think that a task isn't completed just because it isn't perfect. Also, this mentality can prevent you from starting something. Not just starting, but even completing it as well. Instead of chasing perfection, you should focus on being better and completing the task.

Focusing on the result

If you are putting something off, then you can change your thinking with an emphasis on the effect. Think about how wonderful you will feel when the work is done, and you have done it well. Visualization is a great tool, and it will help in reducing the anxiety that you might be feeling before getting started. A positive mentality makes it easier to get things done.

Forgiving yourself

If you slip up and end up procrastinating, don't beat yourself up about it. You might think that punishing yourself about it will prevent you from doing it again in the future. This certainly isn't the case. Instead, it will simply start the vicious circle of procrastination all over again. If you slip up, just let that instance go and start focusing on getting your work done.

Catastrophizing

One of the main reasons for procrastination is that many people tend to make a big deal out of something. When you start thinking about how tough, boring, or painful it will be to get the task done; then you will start postponing it. Well, regardless of how difficult a task is, getting it done will not harm you. On the other hand, procrastination will just create more stress. It is about getting things in perspective. Keep telling yourself that you will be able to get through it and you actually will.

Procrastination

Check your calendar

Tasks, projects or chores that will be done "when I have time," often, are left as it is. Make a schedule. Plan your days in such a manner that you will be able to work on the project without it clashing with any other significant commitments. When you allocate some time for doing a thing, then you will be able to get it done.

No time for excuses

"I was not in the mood," "I work better when there's a deadline set" and so on. These are just excuses that we keep making for putting something on hold. You just need to get done with yourself. Don't kid yourself into thinking that these are valid reasons. They are just excuses and stop making these excuses.

Getting a partner is helpful

You should establish deadlines for completing a project. Once you do this, find yourself a partner who will help you in being accountable. It could be a simple promise that you have made to your boss or your client about completing a job by a particular date. Or it could even be a coach who will help you stay on track and not lose your focus. Your partner or buddy will help in making sure that you aren't procrastinating and that you are getting things done in a timely fashion. After a while, you won't need someone else to tell you all this. You will be able to do this on your own.

Chapter Four:

Ways To Enhance Productivity

Productivity doesn't have to be restricted to just your professional life. You can be productive in your day-to-day life as well. Being productive will help in accomplishing more and will leave you feeling contented with yourself. In this chapter, you will learn about the different things that you can do for improving your productivity.

Make a to-do list

Making a to-do list is quite helpful. Take a sheet of paper and list down all the things that you have to do on that particular day. You can do this as soon as you wake up in the morning, or you can make your to-do list on the previous night before going to bed. So, when you wake up in the morning, you will have a sense of direction, and you will know what needs to be accomplished by the end of the day. A to-do list also helps in relieving your anxiety about a particular task. A to-do list is extremely handy, and it will help in making sure that you don't forget anything. For instance, if you have to spend about three hours attending meetings and have eight hours of work after that, then it is unlikely that you will be able to get everything done. A to-do list will simply tell you the number of things you will need to get done, but it won't tell you the number of hours you have for completing these tasks.

Procrastination

If you want your to-do list to be of some value, then you will need to make sure that you have allocated your time for different things. When you have allocated your time for different tasks, then you will realize the tasks that are feasible and the ones that aren't. By doing this, you will be able to prioritize your day and get started with the tasks that are a priority and leave the rest for later. Setting goals will not do you any good if you don't monitor your progress. Keep an eye on your performance and see what you have done so far in the day. If you feel that you are lagging behind, then you can tweak your goals in such a way that you will be able to get done with your work.

Create a reward system

Always create a reward system for yourself. Regardless of whether you have completed a small or a big task, you should always reward yourself for completing your work. The reward system doesn't have to be an elaborate one. For instance, you can treat yourself to a cup of coffee once you have reviewed your emails in the morning. This small reward will provide you with the necessary motivation to complete the task.

Breaking up your workday

Breaks are essential, and you will need a couple of breaks while you are working. It is quite difficult to work efficiently for prolonged periods of time without any breaks. Try breaking up your tasks into smaller and manageable parts. This will make it easier to complete the task, and it will provide you with a sense of accomplishment. If you have to work for 6 hours on any given day, then schedule a break for yourself after every two hours. A small break will make you feel fresh, and it will improve your ability to concentrate as well.

Chapter Four: Ways To Enhance Productivity

Don't indulge in any activities that would waste your time

Avoid or try reducing the time you spend indulging in any addictive time-wasting activities. It could be anything. Even something as simple as playing a game on your phone can be quite addictive or constantly checking your social media feed. These activities will not help you in accomplishing anything, and they just eat into your working hours. Set certain limits. You can do these things while on a break, but not while you are working. Get your work done and then you have got plenty of time for all the other activities.

Get as much done as possible

It is always better to get as many things done as possible as early in the day as you possibly can. It is easier concentrate and work efficiently in the morning, or that's the case for most people. The more you delay it, it worse it will get. Start your day with a bang and this will give you the required boost to keep going. Then you can have the rest of the night for unwinding without feeling like you haven't been productive the whole day. You should get to the important things first. Your ability to concentrate is higher when you arrive at your workplace. So, make the most of it. Don't spend all this precious energy on going through your emails! Checking your email early in the morning will not only distract you, but it is a waste of your energy as well.

Tackle the tough tasks first

There will always be a couple of tasks that you think are tough. It is a good idea to get these tasks out of the way as soon as you possibly can. Don't keep these tasks on hold. Once you are done with these tasks, the rest will be relatively simpler.

Procrastination

Showcasing your success

This will provide you with the necessary motivation and momentum to keep going. Whenever you achieve a goal, pat yourself on the back and enjoy your success. You can strike that task off your to-do list. You can perhaps call your significant other and tell him/her about your accomplishment.

Discuss your goals with someone

When you tell someone about your goals, you are unknowingly increasing your accountability. It is likely that you will finish a task if you have already told someone about it. You get to decide who you want to discuss it with. Accountability towards someone else will make you want to complete the task on hand.

Being realistic

It is okay to take a break. Everyone needs a break. If a particular task seems to be difficult or even frustrating, then take a break and clear your mind. You can get back to it after a while. In the meanwhile, you can focus on something else. Taking a break will help you in getting a better perspective of how things should be, and this is quite helpful when you are working. Be realistic when you are planning your schedule. You are human too, and you won't be able to function for prolonged periods of time without it affecting your overall productivity.

Setting goals should become a habit

The thought of having to make a to-do list daily does sound cumbersome. Find a method that works well for you. The aim is to set goals. The method that you employ to accomplish this task doesn't matter. What matters is the fact that you have

Chapter Four: Ways To Enhance Productivity

managed to set some goals for yourself. While setting goals, make sure that the goals are small and achievable. This will help you in measuring your progress and also push you to complete tasks. Setting goals is a positive activity and helps in improving your productivity. Make it a habit of setting goals for yourself. Doing this regularly will help in improving your level of confidence as well and providing you with some sense of control over your life. It helps in getting things in motion when you have predefined goals. Make sure that the goals you have set for yourself are specific and not vague.

Start the day with exercise

Try starting your day with some form of exercise. This will get your juices flowing and will make you feel pumped up for the day ahead. The endorphins released during exercising will elevate your mood as well. You don't have to go to the gym; you can engage in any physical activity of your choice. You can go for a walk, jog, do yoga, or anything else that you feel like doing. The aim is to exercise for at least 15 minutes every morning.

Have a glass of lemon water

You can provide your body with a nice boost of energy in the morning by having a glass of lemon water. You will feel refreshed, physically and mentally as well. Adding a couple of drops of lime juice will improve the ability of your body to absorb nutrients. Have a glass of this as soon as you wake up and give yourself a gap of 30 minutes before you eat something. If your weight is about 150 pounds, then drink half a glass of warm water and juice of a small lemon. If you weight is on the other side of 150 pounds, then increase the quantity to a bigger lemon. Mix the lemon juice with water; if you don't do this, then the acid in the lemon might hurt your teeth.

Procrastination

No gadgets early in the morning

In today's world, there are plenty of gadgets to keep yourself distracted like cell phones, tablets and laptops. It is a common habit to wake up in the morning and immediately check your texts, emails and social media updates. Your mind tends to be fresh, and your ability to concentrate is quite high in the morning. When you squander away this energy on trivial things, you are hurting your productivity. Do something that will set a positive and a relaxing tone for the rest of the day. Don't reach for your gadgets first thing in the morning. Exercise, meditate, or just sit and read the newspaper for a while. You have got plenty of time in the day for checking all these gadgets. So, do it later. If you want your day to be productive, it is necessary that it starts out well.

Don't skip your breakfast

Having breakfast is incredibly important! It is, in fact, the most important meal of the day. People who tend to have breakfast on a regular basis are likely to be less obese, and they have better levels of blood sugar. Having breakfast in the morning will ensure that you have sufficient energy to get through the day and your hunger pangs will be kept at bay as well. Having a healthy breakfast will help in giving you plenty of energy, it will help in improving your short-term energy, and will improve your ability to concentrate as well.

It is incredibly important that you start your day well. However, this is just the beginning. You will need to maintain this momentum even after reaching your workplace. That's the only way in which you will be able to increase your productivity. Here are a few things that you can do for improving your productivity at work as well.

Cleaning up your workspace

It might seem like quite a task to clean your workspace as soon as you get to work. However, this small step can help in improving your ability to concentrate. Working in a space that is cluttered and messy will simply lead to unnecessary distractions. This will pull your attention away from all the important things. If your workstation is clean and organized, you will be able to concentrate better.

Saying no

"No" is quite a powerful word and it can help you in protecting your valuable time. When you have got to say "no," just say it. Don't make use of phrases like "I am not sure," "I don't think I will be able to" and so on. If you won't be able to take on any additional commitments or if you feel that you have got a lot of work to do, then don't take on any new commitments. Just say no. If you get stuck with something that you won't be able to do, then this will just create additional stress, pressure and just burn you out eventually. Learn how to say no, and this will help in improving your productivity.

Conclusion

I would like to thank you once again for purchasing this book.

By overcoming procrastination, you can increase your overall productivity and start working towards achieving your goals. Procrastination can become quite a big hurdle in your life if left unchecked. Unknowingly, procrastination can get a firm grip over you and stop you from functioning effectively in your daily life. There are a couple of simple strategies that you can make use of for overcoming procrastination and for becoming more productive. By making the small changes that have been explained in this book, you will be able to make the most of all the opportunities that come your way.

Finally, if you enjoyed this book, then I'd like to ask you for a favor, would you be kind enough to leave a review for this book on Amazon? It'd be greatly appreciated!

Click here to leave a review for this book on Amazon!

Thank you and good luck!

www.ingramcontent.com/pod-product-compliance
Lightning Source LLC
Chambersburg PA
CBHW050037230526
45470CB00003B/1321